Welcome!

Are you ready to get your novel up and running?

No matter where you're starting from, planning a novel is a simple process... if you have a process.

Without a process it's *hard*.

Simple doesn't necessarily mean easy though - you still need to come up with story ideas and put them together. This workbook provides the process and space to get it all in order.

All you need to do is fill in the blanks. Simple, if not easy.

Inside you'll find three templates, enough for for three standalone novels or two practice runs and a final.

Once you've filled in the blanks you'll have a complete outline that's comprehensive enough to cover all the story bases you need to write your novel, with enough space left over for plenty of creativity.

When you're done planning, use it as your 'once source of truth' reference book.

Good luck with your epic masterpiece!

Your opinion matters to me!

Please let me know what you think of this workbook by leaving a review where you purchased it.

If you have any improvements you'd like to see, email your ideas to Chris@ChrisAndrews.me

Enjoy!

Chris

Using This Workbook

This workbook is a companion to *Character and Structure: An Unholy Alliance,* which delivers all the core knowledge professional storytellers use for developing and troubleshooting stories, and shows you how to use it.

You don't have to have read *Character and Structure: An Unholy Alliance* to use this workbook, but you'll certainly get more from it if you have.

If you already have a solid understanding of storytelling you're good to go. If not, you can get clarity on some of the terms used with simple internet search.

This workbook is easy enough for anyone with a basic grasp of storytelling to utilise it, yet in-depth enough to provide everything you need to outline a complex novel or three.

Although this workbook is based around a simple process, you don't have to be a slave to it. Feel free to repurpose anything you like. It's your workbook, after all.

Otherwise, it's a handy place to keep your ideas together, and it makes for a great teaching aid.

That's it. It's now time to get started.

Simply fill in the blanks and you'll have everything you need to hit all the major story points necessary for writing your novel, with plenty of room for additional scenes, chapters, dialogue snippets, and notes.

Assumptions

Although storytelling is based on knowledge and audience expectations, all novels differ in focus, genre, length, number of chapters and scenes etc.

Because of that I've had to make some assumptions. To accommodate those assumptions and add flexibility, I've added extra sections with indicative headings you can use in any way you like.

Assumption 1. Your novel is perfectly balanced in terms of the number of chapters per quarter (a stupid assumption, but we have to start somewhere). While the length of each section needs to be about the same for a well-balanced story, the number of chapters and scenes can vary drastically.

Assumption 2. Your novel therefore is going to have exactly 40 chapters – 10 per quarter (the numbers work really well, but there's room for extra chapters if you need more – or simply ignore those you don't need). If they're all used, it works out to be 2000-3000 words per chapter, making your novel 80,000-120,000 words in total. That's approximately what publishers look for. Feel free to adjust that in any way you like.

Assumption 3. You already have a reasonable grasp of storytelling from reading *Character and Structure: An Unholy Alliance* or through your own research. Because of that assumed knowledge, the terms used within aren't explained in depth. It's not hard to look them up though.

Good luck! I'm looking forward to hearing about your success!

Novel Structure Diagram

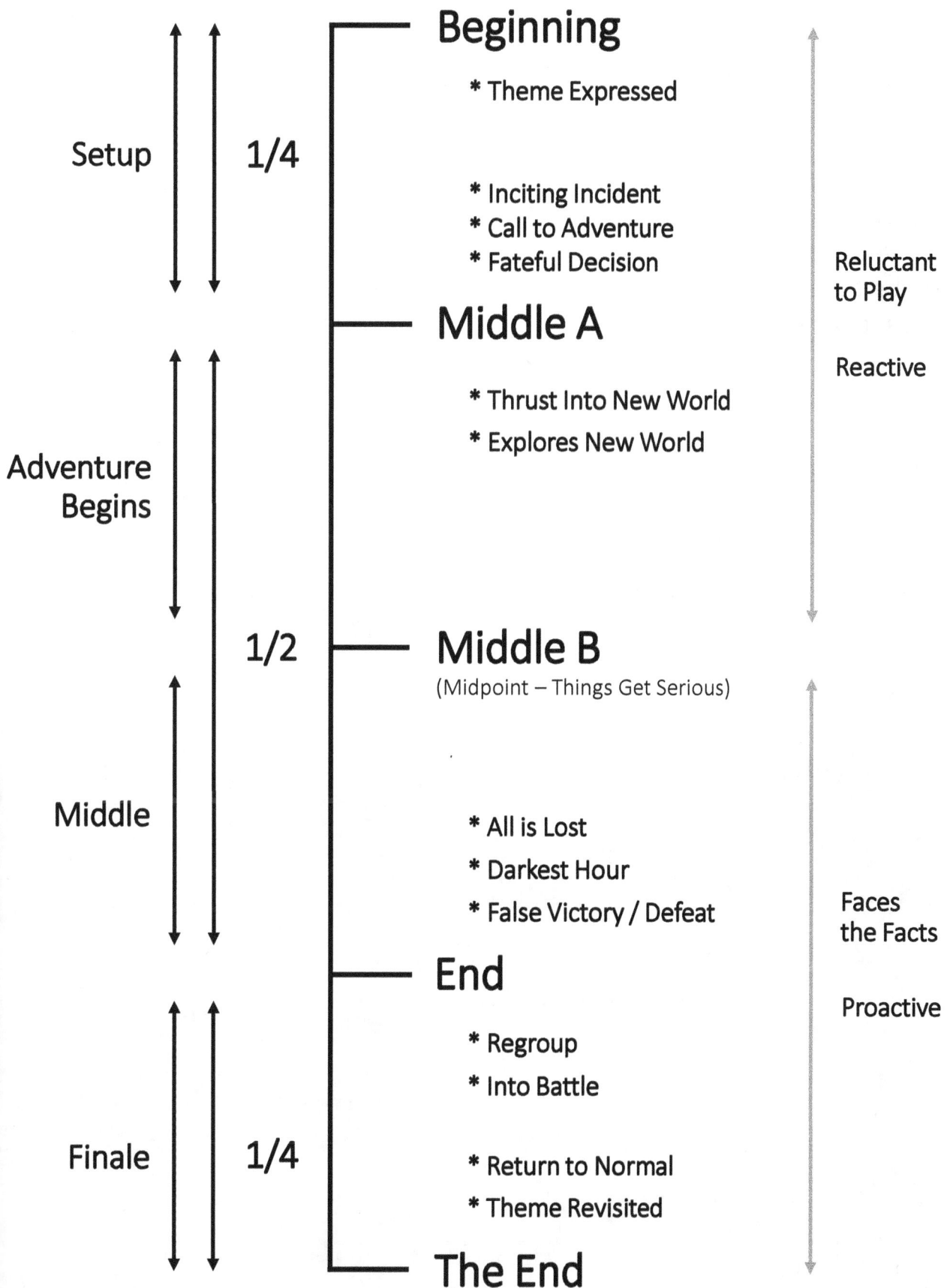

Setup — 1/4

Beginning

* Theme Expressed

* Inciting Incident
* Call to Adventure
* Fateful Decision

Middle A

* Thrust Into New World
* Explores New World

Reluctant to Play

Reactive

Adventure Begins

Middle — 1/2

Middle B
(Midpoint – Things Get Serious)

* All is Lost
* Darkest Hour
* False Victory / Defeat

End

* Regroup
* Into Battle

Faces the Facts

Proactive

Finale — 1/4

* Return to Normal
* Theme Revisited

The End

Novel Project 1

Title:

Subtitle:

Story overview / blurb:
(in general terms
describe the story
you want to write)

Details

Genre:

Story Premise:
(25 Words of Less)

Primary Theme:
(Question or Statement)

Why will anyone care?

First Half:
(What happens?)

What problems
will be raised?

What questions
will be raised?

Second Half:
(What happens?)

How will you resolve
these problems?

How will you answer
these questions?

Unresolved problems
or questions for sequels?

Story Overview

First Quarter
Setup

Second Quarter
Adventure Begins

Third Quarter
Things Get Serious

Fourth Quarter
Resolution

Storylines

Primary Storyline:

Introduction:

Resolution:

How it contributes to Primary storyline:

Subplot 1 (i.e., Romance)

Introduction:

Resolution:

How it contributes to Primary storyline:

Subplot 2

Introduction:

Resolution:

How it contributes to Primary storyline:

Subplot 3

Introduction:

Resolution:

How it contributes to Primary storyline:

Subplot 4

Introduction:

Resolution:

How it contributes to Primary storyline:

Character & Structure Points

Place into chapters in order of appearance – the chapter numbers are a guide only.

Hook/opening image:
(Beginning - Chapter 1)

Theme expressed:
(Beginning - Chapter 1 or 2)

Call to Adventure:
(Beginning - Chapter 6-10)

Fateful Decision:
(Beginning - Chapter 9-10)

Thrust into New World:
(Middle A - The Adventure Begins.
How will they react?)

Explores New World:
(Middle A - Show Contrast With What
They're Familiar With)

All Is Lost:
(Middle B - Chapter 26-30)

Darkest Hour:
(Middle B - Chapter 26-30)

False Victory/Defeat:
(Middle B - Chapter 26-30)

Regroup:
(End - Chapter 31-35)

Into Battle:
(End - Chapter 32-38)

Return to Normal:
(End - Chapter 36-40)

Theme Revisited:
(End - Chapter 39-40)

Beginning – Chapter Overview

Chapter 1:

Chapter 2:

Chapter 3:

Chapter 4:

Chapter 5:

Chapter 6:

Chapter 7:

Chapter 8:

Chapter 9:

Chapter 10:

Middle (A) - Chapter Overview

Chapter 11:

Chapter 12:

Chapter 13:

Chapter 14:

Chapter 15:

Chapter 16:

Chapter 17:

Chapter 18:

Chapter 19:

Chapter 20:

Middle (B) - Chapter Overview

Chapter 21:

Chapter 22:

Chapter 23:

Chapter 24:

Chapter 25:

Chapter 26:

Chapter 27:

Chapter 28:

Chapter 29:

Chapter 30:

The End – Chapter Overview

Chapter 31:

Chapter 32:

Chapter 33:

Chapter 34:

Chapter 35:

Chapter 36:

Chapter 37:

Chapter 38:

Chapter 39:

Chapter 40:

Scene Ideas or Extra Chapters

Scene Ideas or Extra Chapters

Dialogue Ideas

Notes

Notes

Notes

Novel Project 2

Title:

Subtitle:

Story overview / blurb:
(in general terms
describe the story
you want to write)

Details

Genre:

Story Premise:
(25 Words of Less)

Primary Theme:
(Question or Statement)

Why will anyone care?

First Half:
(What happens?)

What problems
will be raised?

What questions
will be raised?

Second Half:
(What happens?)

How will you resolve
these problems?

How will you answer
these questions?

Unresolved problems
or questions for sequels?

Story Overview

First Quarter
Setup

Second Quarter
Adventure Begins

Third Quarter
Things Get Serious

Fourth Quarter
Resolution

Storylines

Primary Storyline:

Introduction:

Resolution:

How it contributes to Primary storyline:

Subplot 1 (i.e., Romance)

Introduction:

Resolution:

How it contributes to Primary storyline:

Subplot 2

Introduction:

Resolution:

How it contributes to Primary storyline:

Subplot 3

Introduction:

Resolution:

How it contributes to Primary storyline:

Subplot 4

Introduction:

Resolution:

How it contributes to Primary storyline:

Character & Structure Points

Place into chapters in order of appearance – the chapter numbers are a guide only.

Hook/opening image:
(Beginning - Chapter 1)

Theme expressed:
(Beginning - Chapter 1 or 2)

Call to Adventure:
(Beginning - Chapter 6-10)

Fateful Decision:
(Beginning - Chapter 9-10)

Thrust into New World:
(Middle A - The Adventure Begins.
How will they react?)

Explores New World:
(Middle A - Show Contrast With What
They're Familiar With)

All Is Lost:
(Middle B - Chapter 26-30)

Darkest Hour:
(Middle B - Chapter 26-30)

False Victory/Defeat:
(Middle B - Chapter 26-30)

Regroup:
(End - Chapter 31-35)

Into Battle:
(End - Chapter 32-38)

Return to Normal:
(End - Chapter 36-40)

Theme Revisited:
(End - Chapter 39-40)

Beginning – Chapter Overview

Chapter 1:

Chapter 2:

Chapter 3:

Chapter 4:

Chapter 5:

Chapter 6:

Chapter 7:

Chapter 8:

Chapter 9:

Chapter 10:

Middle (A) - Chapter Overview

Chapter 11:

Chapter 12:

Chapter 13:

Chapter 14:

Chapter 15:

Chapter 16:

Chapter 17:

Chapter 18:

Chapter 19:

Chapter 20:

Middle (B) - Chapter Overview

Chapter 21:

Chapter 22:

Chapter 23:

Chapter 24:

Chapter 25:

Chapter 26:

Chapter 27:

Chapter 28:

Chapter 29:

Chapter 30:

The End – Chapter Overview

Chapter 31:

Chapter 32:

Chapter 33:

Chapter 34:

Chapter 35:

Chapter 36:

Chapter 37:

Chapter 38:

Chapter 39:

Chapter 40:

Scene Ideas or Extra Chapters

Scene Ideas or Extra Chapters

Dialogue Ideas

Notes

Notes

Notes

Novel Project 3

Title:

Subtitle:

Story overview / blurb:
(in general terms
describe the story
you want to write)

Details

Genre:

Story Premise:
(25 Words of Less)

Primary Theme:
(Question or Statement)

Why will anyone care?

First Half:
(What happens?)

What problems
will be raised?

What questions
will be raised?

Second Half:
(What happens?)

How will you resolve
these problems?

How will you answer
these questions?

Unresolved problems
or questions for sequels?

Story Overview

First Quarter
Setup

Second Quarter
Adventure Begins

Third Quarter
Things Get Serious

Fourth Quarter
Resolution

Storylines

Primary Storyline:

Introduction:

Resolution:

How it contributes to Primary storyline:

Subplot 1 (i.e., Romance)

Introduction:

Resolution:

How it contributes to Primary storyline:

Subplot 2

Introduction:

Resolution:

How it contributes to Primary storyline:

Subplot 3

Introduction:

Resolution:

How it contributes to Primary storyline:

Subplot 4

Introduction:

Resolution:

How it contributes to Primary storyline:

Character & Structure Points

Place into chapters in order of appearance – the chapter numbers are a guide only.

Hook/opening image:
(Beginning - Chapter 1)

Theme expressed:
(Beginning - Chapter 1 or 2)

Call to Adventure:
(Beginning - Chapter 6-10)

Fateful Decision:
(Beginning - Chapter 9-10)

Thrust into New World:
(Middle A - The Adventure Begins.
How will they react?)

Explores New World:
(Middle A - Show Contrast With What
They're Familiar With)

All Is Lost:
(Middle B - Chapter 26-30)

Darkest Hour:
(Middle B - Chapter 26-30)

False Victory/Defeat:
(Middle B - Chapter 26-30)

Regroup:
(End - Chapter 31-35)

Into Battle:
(End - Chapter 32-38)

Return to Normal:
(End - Chapter 36-40)

Theme Revisited:
(End - Chapter 39-40)

Beginning – Chapter Overview

Chapter 1:

Chapter 2:

Chapter 3:

Chapter 4:

Chapter 5:

Chapter 6:

Chapter 7:

Chapter 8:

Chapter 9:

Chapter 10:

Middle (A) - Chapter Overview

Chapter 11:

Chapter 12:

Chapter 13:

Chapter 14:

Chapter 15:

Chapter 16:

Chapter 17:

Chapter 18:

Chapter 19:

Chapter 20:

Middle (B) - Chapter Overview

Chapter 21:

Chapter 22:

Chapter 23:

Chapter 24:

Chapter 25:

Chapter 26:

Chapter 27:

Chapter 28:

Chapter 29:

Chapter 30:

The End – Chapter Overview

Chapter 31:

Chapter 32:

Chapter 33:

Chapter 34:

Chapter 35:

Chapter 36:

Chapter 37:

Chapter 38:

Chapter 39:

Chapter 40:

Scene Ideas or Extra Chapters

Scene Ideas or Extra Chapters

Dialogue Ideas

Notes

Notes

Notes

Thoughts?

Your opinion matters to me.

Please leave a review wherever you purchased this workbook.

Reviews let people know the book's worth their time.

Thank you, in advance.

Chris

Stay in Touch

If you want to stay in touch, I have a blog where you can keep up to date with my projects and subscribe to my newsletter:

- http://www.chrisandrews.me

Wishing you the best of luck and success,

Chris Andrews